Ladybird Readers

Goodbye, Cricket

Notes to teachers, parents, and carers

The *Ladybird Readers* Beginner level helps young language learners to become familiar with key conversational phrases in English. The language introduced has clear real-life applications, giving children the tools to hold their first conversations in English.

This book focuses on different ways of saying goodbye, and introduces insect names in English.

There are some activities to do in this book. They will help children practice these skills:

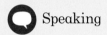 Speaking    Listening*   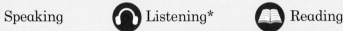 Reading

*To complete these activities, listen to the audio downloads available at **www.ladybirdeducation.co.uk**

Series Editor: Sorrel Pitts
Chants by Sorrel Pitts

LADYBIRD BOOKS

UK | USA | Canada | Ireland | Australia
India | New Zealand | South Africa

Ladybird Books is part of the Penguin Random House group of companies
whose addresses can be found at global.penguinrandomhouse.com.
www.penguin.co.uk   www.puffin.co.uk   www.ladybird.co.uk

Penguin
Random House
UK

Text inspired by *The Very Quiet Cricket* by Eric Carle, first published in Great Britain by Hamish Hamilton Ltd, 1997
This version first published by Ladybird Books 2024
001

Printed in China

The authorized representative in the EEA is Penguin Random House Ireland, Morrison Chambers, 32 Nassau Street, Dublin D02 YH68

A CIP catalogue record for this book is available from the British Library

ISBN: 978-0-241-58769-0

All correspondence to:
Ladybird Books
Penguin Random House Children's
One Embassy Gardens, 8 Viaduct Gardens, London SW11 7BW

Ladybird Readers

Goodbye, Cricket

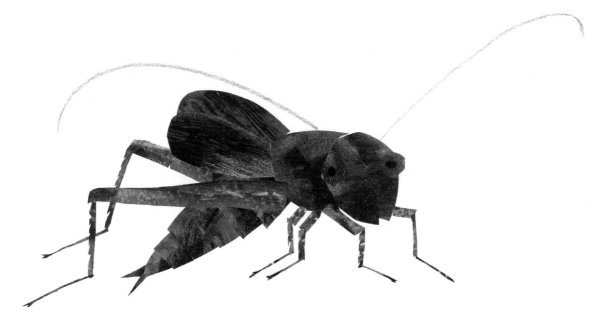

Inspired by
The Very Quiet Cricket
by Eric Carle

"Goodbye, Cricket!"

"Goodbye, Worm."

"Bye, Cricket!"

"Bye, Spittlebug."

"See you later, Cricket!"

"See you later, Bee."

"Bye-bye, Cricket!"

"Bye-bye, Dragonfly."

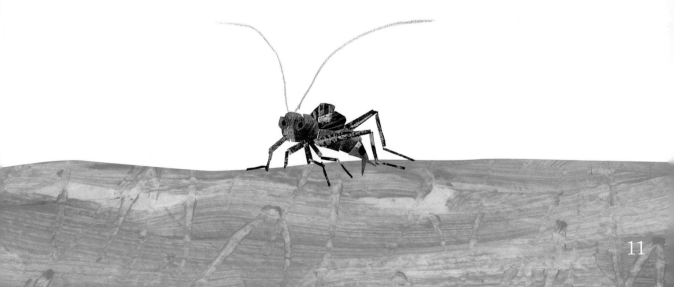

"Goodnight, Cricket!"

12

"Goodnight, Moth."

1 **Talk with a friend.**

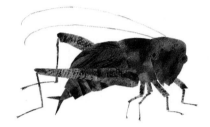

Goodbye!

Goodbye!

See you later!

See you later!

Goodnight!

Goodnight!

2 **Listen and read. Match.** 🎧 📖

1 "Goodbye, Worm."

2 "Bye, Spittlebug."

3 "See you later, Bee."

4 "Bye-bye, Dragonfly."

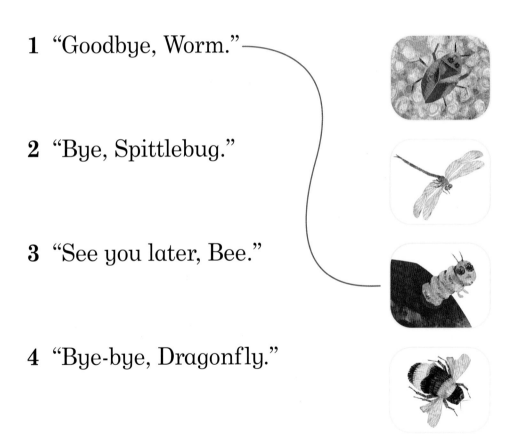

3 Read and clap!

Goodbye! Goodbye!
Goodbye, Cricket!

Bye-bye! Bye-bye!
Bye-bye, Cricket!

See you later! See you later!
See you later, Cricket!

Goodnight! Goodnight!
Goodnight, Cricket!